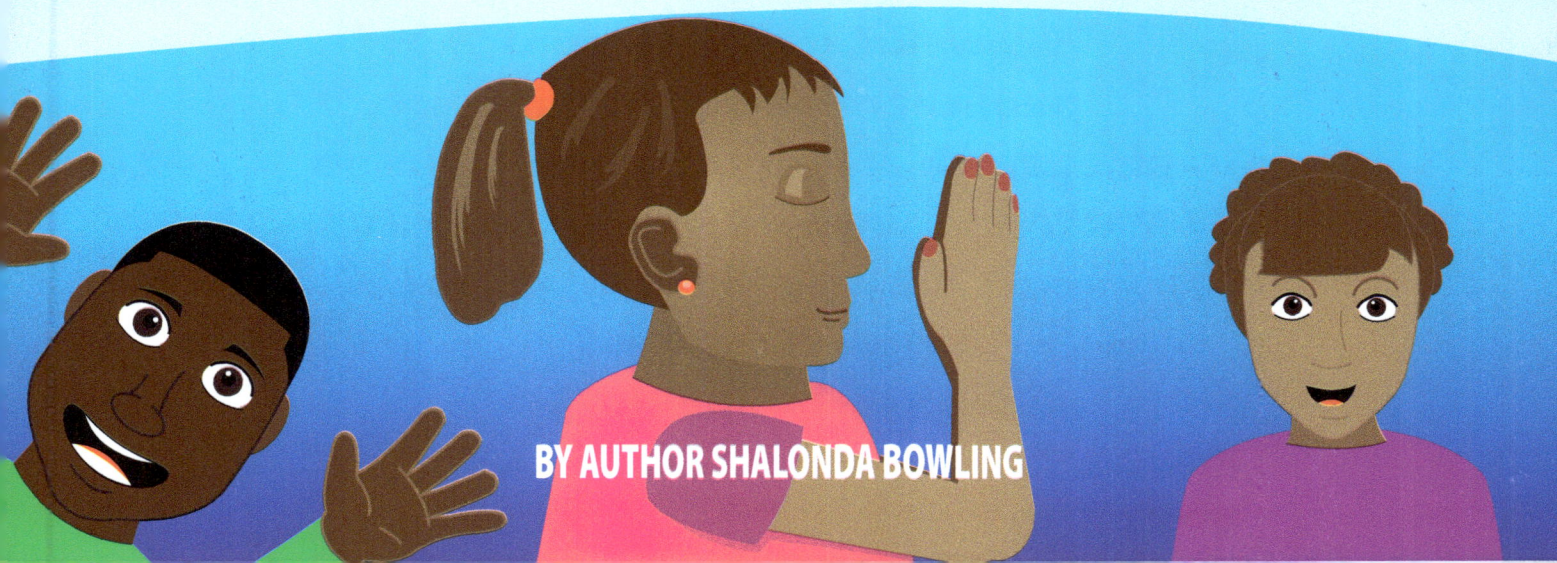

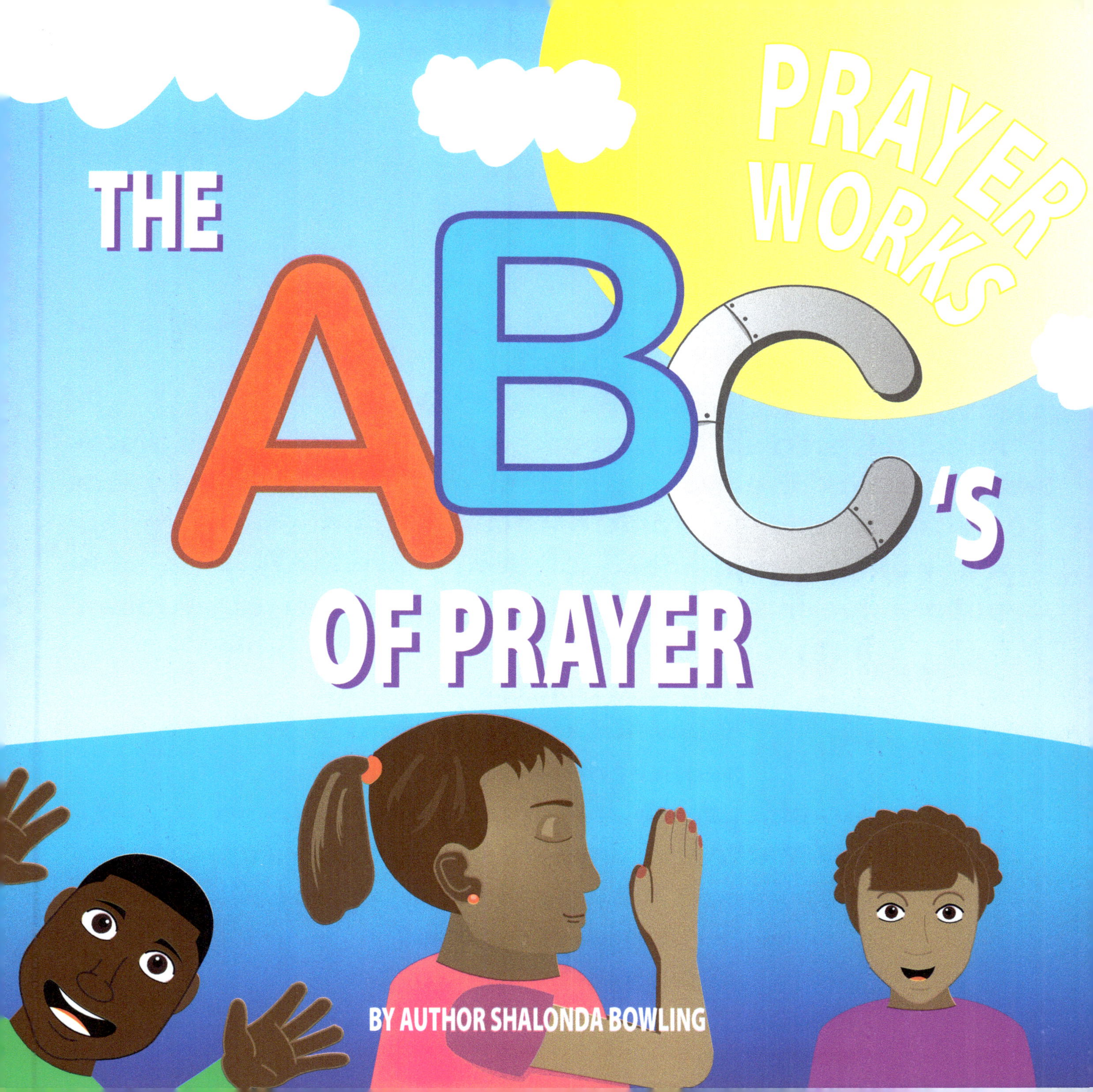
PRAYER WORKS
THE ABC's OF PRAYER
BY AUTHOR SHALONDA BOWLING

Copyright
THE ABC'S OF PRAYER
All rights reserved. No part of this publication may be reproduced, stored in a retrieval system, or transmitted in any form or by any means-electronic, mechanical, photocopy, recording or any other-except brief quotations in printed reviews, without prior permission of the publisher. Bible verses are taken from various translations of the Holy Bible.
Anointed Hands Publishing
www.ninamotivates.info
publishernina@gmail.com
Graphics and Marketing: Shawn Robinson
727 Marketing: www.727marketingllc.com
Copyright© 2021, by Nina Motivates LLC,
All rights reserved
ISBN: 978-1-7365910-2-4

Ask

ABIGAIL TALKS TO GOD IN PRAYER EVERY DAY BECAUSE SHE UNDERSTANDS THAT SHE CAN ASK GOD FOR EVERYTHING THAT SHE NEEDS.

MATTHEW 7:7 KJV
ASK AND IT SHALL BE GIVEN YOU; SEEK, AND YE SHALL FIND; KNOCK, AND IT SHALL BE OPENED UNTO YOU.

BRANDON BELIEVED THAT GOD COULD HEAR HIM WHEN HE PRAYED.

Believe

MATTHEW 9:28 KJV
BELIEVE YE THAT I AM ABLE TO DO THIS?

COREY IS VERY STRONG WILLED AND COURAGEOUS BECAUSE HE KNOWS THAT GOD IS ALWAYS WITH HIM.

Courage

ISAIAH 41:6
BE OF GOOD COURAGE.

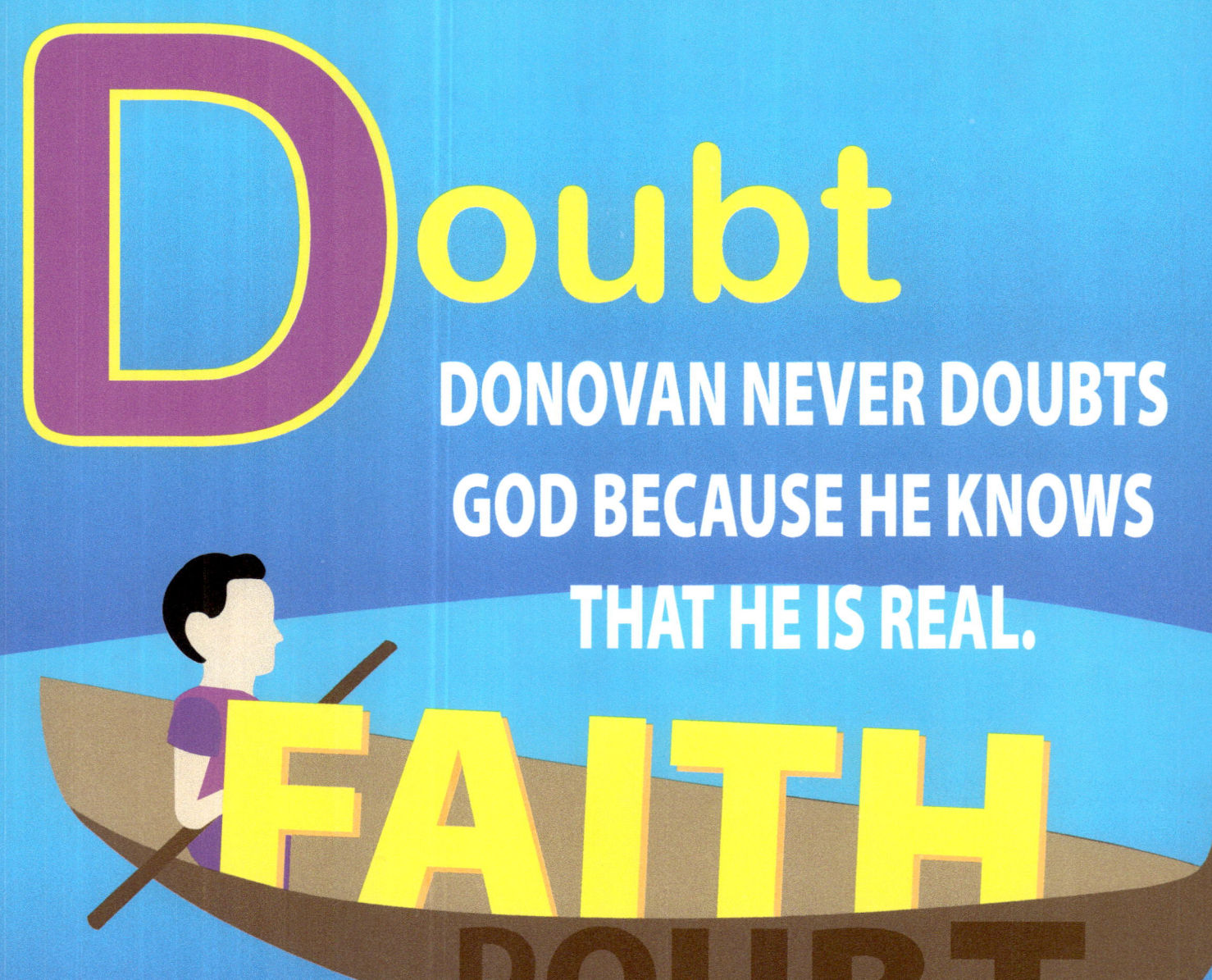

EMILY USED HER IMAGINATION TO SEE WHAT SHE PRAYED FOR UNTIL IT HAPPENED.

Expect

PROVERBS 23:18 KJV
YOUR EXPECTATION SHALL NOT BE CUT OFF.

Faith

Faith was confident that she could trust God.

Matthew 9:22 NLT
Your faith has made you well.

GREGORY ALWAYS REMEMBERED TO TELL GOD THANK YOU AT THE BEGINNING OF HIS PRAYER AND AT THE END.

EPHESIANS 5:20 KJV
GIVING THANKS ALWAYS FOR ALL THINGS UNTO GOD THE FATHER IN THE NAME OF OUR LORD JESUS CHRIST.

GRATEFUL

IRVIN OFTEN PRAYED FOR HIS FRIENDS.

INTERCEDE

1 TIMOTHY 2:1 ESV
I URGE THAT SUPPLICATIONS, PRAYERS, INTERCESSIONS, AND THANKSGIVINGS BE MADE FOR ALL PEOPLE.

KARSON BOWS DOWN ON HIS KNEES AND PRAYS EVERY NIGHT BEFORE HE GOES TO SLEEP.

PSALMS 95:6
COME LET US PSALMS 95:6 NLT- COME, LET US WORSHIP AND BOW DOWN. LET US KNEEL BEFORE THE LORD OUR MAKER. AND BOW DOWN: LET US KNEEL BEFORE THE LORD OUR MAKER.

KNEEL

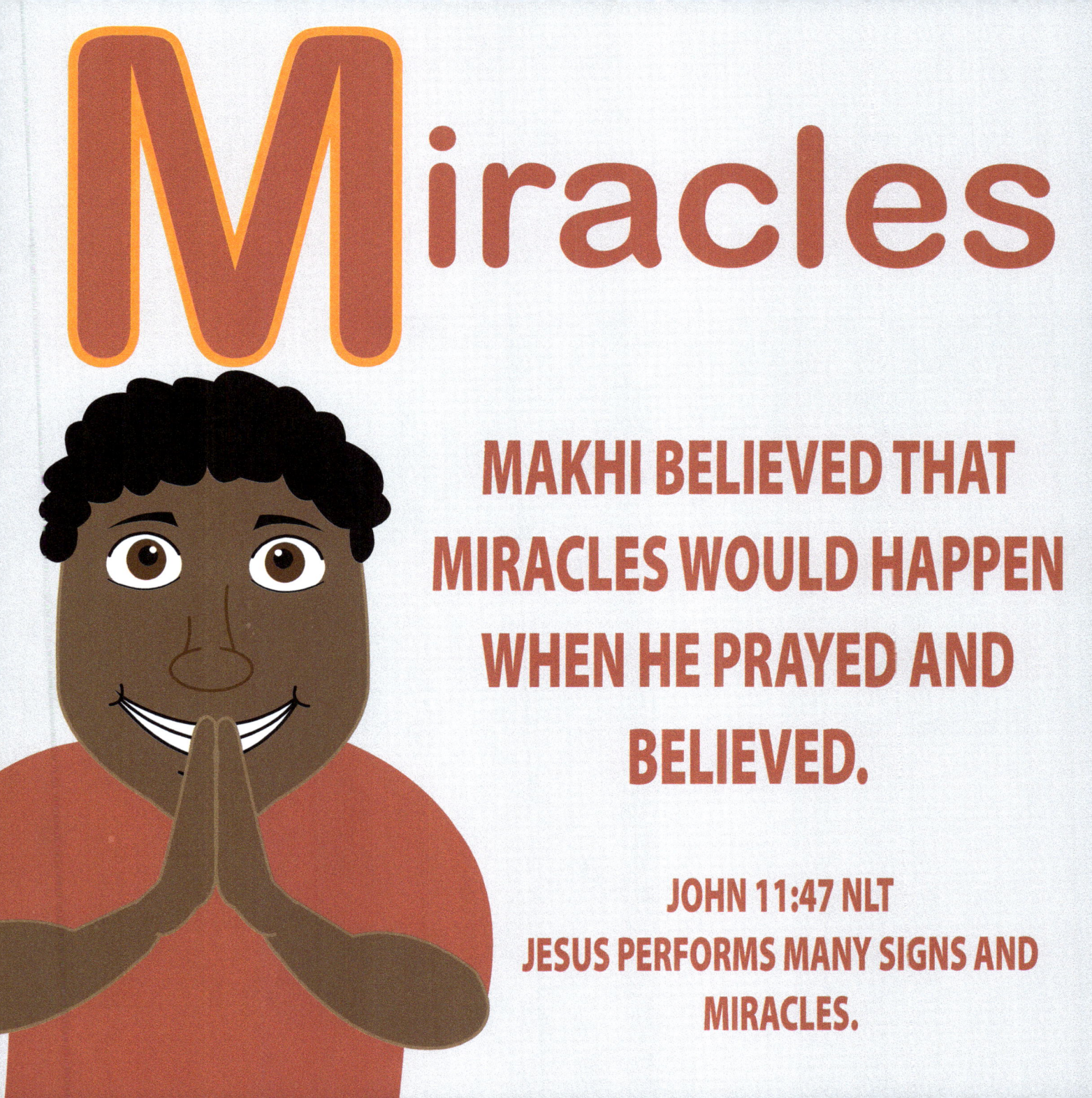

NYIA REMEMBERED WHAT SHE LEARNED IN SUNDAY SCHOOL. WHENEVER SHE PRAYS SHE SHOULD PRAY IN JESUS NAME.

LUKE 10:17
EVEN THE BAD SPIRITS OBEY US WHEN WE USE YOUR NAME

OPEN

OMARI LOVED TO OPEN HIS MOUTH AND PRAY OUT LOUD.

JEREMIAH 29:12 ESV
THEN YOU WILL CALL UPON ME AND COME AND PRAY TO ME, AND I WILL HEAR YOU.

QAADIR'S FRIENDS ASKED HIM WHY DID HE SIT ALONE SO QUIET AFTER BIBLE STUDY. QAADIR ANSWERED, "I SAT QUIETLY TO HEAR GOD TALK TO ME."

Quiet

JOHN 10:27 KJV
MY SHEEP HEAR MY VOICE, AND I KNOW THEM, AND THEY FOLLOW ME.

RENEE PRAYED AND ASKED GOD TO FORGIVE HER FOR DISOBEYING HER MOTHER.

Repent

1 JOHN 1:9 ESV- IF WE ADMIT THAT WE HAVE SINNED AND CONFESS OUR SINS, HE IS FAITHFUL AND JUST AND WILL FORGIVE OUR SINS.

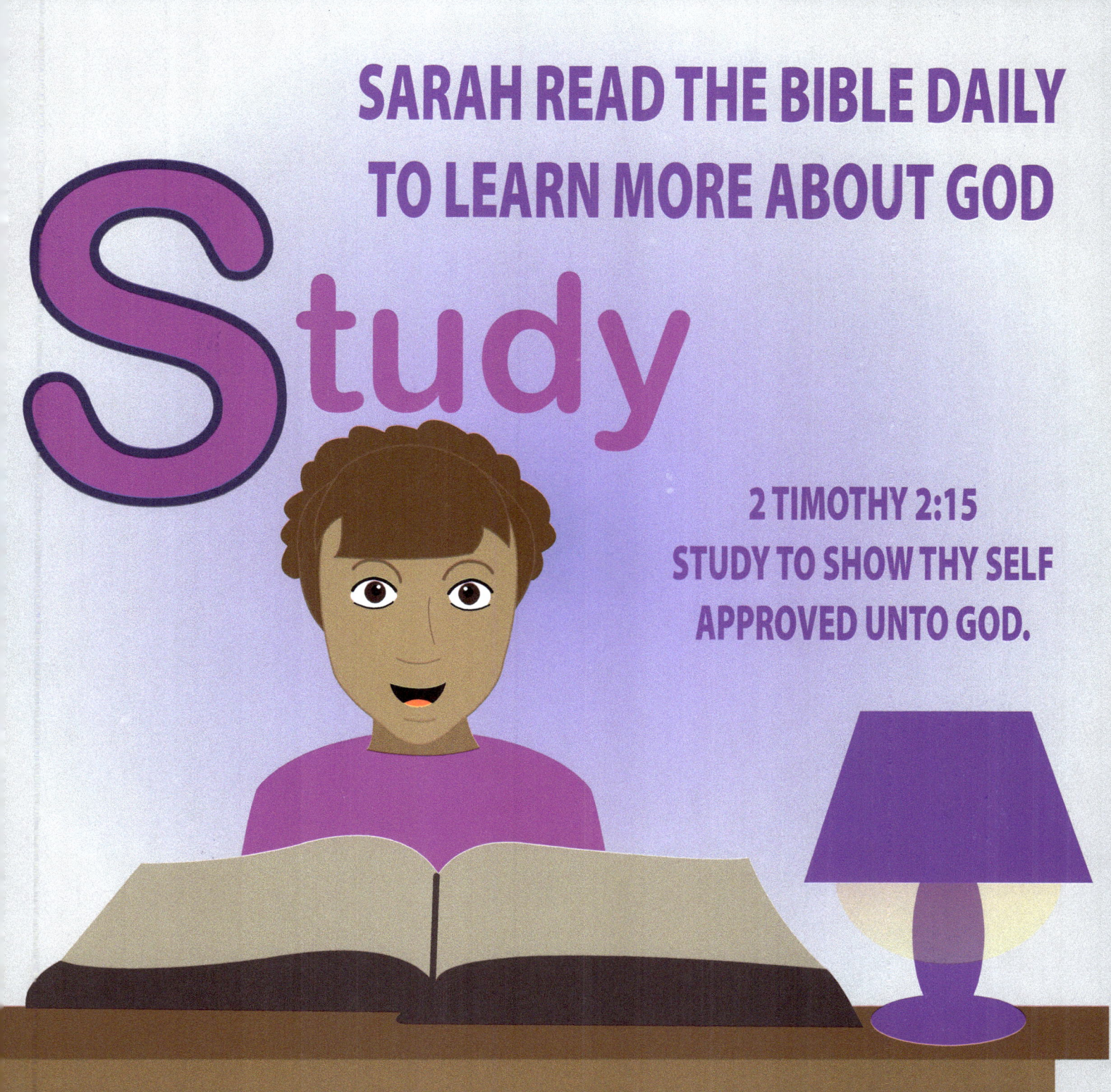

THOMAS WAS RELIEVED TO KNOW THAT HE COULD ALWAYS TRUST GOD AND THAT HE DIDN'T HAVE TO BE AFRAID TO TELL GOD HIS SECRETS.

Trust

PSALMS 62:8
TRUST IN HIM AT ALL TIME YE PEOPLE, POUR OUT YOUR HEART BEFORE HIM: GOD IS A REFUGE FOR US.

URIEL WAS SAD BECAUSE SHE NEEDED MONEY FOR SCHOOL. BUT HER MOTHER ASSURED HER THAT GOD UNDERSTANDS WHO YOU ARE AND WHAT YOU WANT AND NEED.

Understand

ISAIAH 40:28 KJV
THERE IS NO SEARCHING OF GOD'S UNDERSTANDING.

VICTORIA WAS CONCERNED ABOUT HER TEAM LOSING THEIR SOCCER GAME SO SHE PRAYED AND ASKED GOD TO HELP THEM TO WIN. HER TEAM WON 1ST PLACE.

Victory

1 CORINTHIANS 15:57
THANKS BE TO GOD, WHICH GIVETH US THE VICTORY THROUGH OUR LORD AND JESUS CHRIST.

Wait

Walter never hurried to make any choices. He always waited for God to answer his prayers

PSALMS 27:14 NLT
Wait patiently for the Lord. Be brave and courageous. Yes, wait patiently for the Lord.

XAVIER NEVER CARED ABOUT PEOPLE JUDGING HIM BECAUSE HE UNDERSTOOD THAT GOD LOOKS AT YOUR HEART WHEN YOU PRAY.

eXamine

1 SAMUEL 16:7 NLT

PEOPLE JUDGE BY OUTWARD APPEARANCE, BUT THE LORD LOOKS AT THE HEART.

Zealous

Zech was quick to repent because he knows that God loves him and disciplines/corrects him in love.

Revelation 3:19
Those whom I love, I reprove and discipline, so be zealous and repent

Evangelist Shalonda Bowling believes in the power of prayer and has been praying since the age of 10. Learning the importance of prayer at such a young age gave her a desire to teach other kids to pray. Evangelist Bowling has a total of over 20 years of experience working with children. She is a mentor, a VBS teacher and a Sunday school teacher. Working with and helping children is her passion. Evangelist Bowling also has a passion for assisting struggling mothers, as she was gifted assistance in her time of need. Due to this passion, "A Mother's Love Empowerment Services" came forth and was founded in the year 2000. It continues to be a source of spiritual and emotional support for single mothers and women. Affordable daycare services for low-income families is also a service she provides. In 2017 Evangelist Shalonda began sharing online in weekly Prayer & Motivation for Children, along with a Mentoring Group. In 2018 dance troupe ("Dance 360") was formed as a motivational tool through the Art of Dance for young girls. Evangelist Bowling's ministry service includes; Intercession, Teaching, and Evangelism. In 2005 following her answer of "yes" to Almighty God's call upon her life to reach others through the preaching of the Gospel, she was Licensed as a Gospel Minister. Evangelist Bowling's focal scripture and source of encouragement is Isaiah 41:10 "Fear not, for I am with you; Be not dismayed, for I am your God. I will strengthen you, Yes, I will help you, I will uphold you with My righteous right hand." (NKJV)

COME EXPLORE THE ABC'S OF PRAYER! THIS BOOK WILL TEACH CHILDREN HOW TO TALK TO GOD USING THE ALPHABETS FROM A-Z. THERE ARE ILLUSTRATIONS AND SCRIPTURES ALONG THE WAY. CHILDREN WILL HAVE FUN AS THEY LEARN KEY POINTS ON HOW TO PRAY.

AUTHOR SHALONDA BOWLING

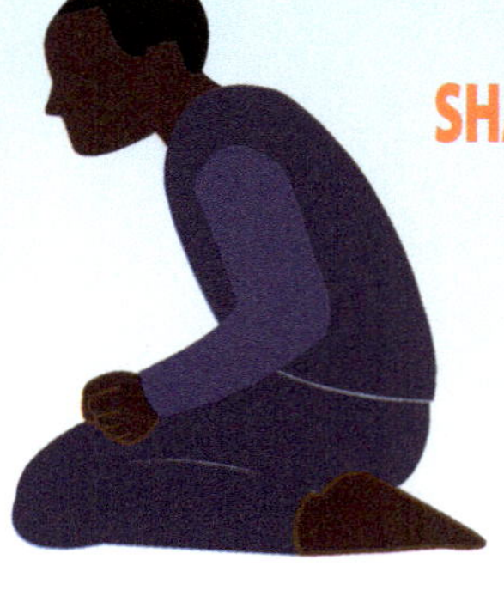

ISBN 978-1-7365910-2-4

$25.00

9 781736 591024

52500>

www.ingramcontent.com/pod-product-compliance
Lightning Source LLC
Chambersburg PA
CBHW061402010526
44119CB00010B/240